THIS BOOK BELONGS TO:

CONTACT INFORMATION

_____

_____

_____

DEDICATION

This Bird Watching Log Book is dedicated to bird enthusiasts, backyard birders, and twitchers who want to keep track of their sightings and observations.

You are my inspiration for producing this book and I'm honored to be a part of your bird watching sessions and future bird sightings.

HOW TO USE THIS BOOK

This Bird Watching Log Book will allow you to accurately document every detail of your bird sightings. It's a great way to track bird activities, weather conditions, habitats, and more.

Here are examples of information for you to fill in and write the details about your experience in this book.

Fill in the following information:

1. Date, Location, And Time - Record information for the day of the sighting.

2. Weather - Use this space to circle or color the icons for the weather.

3. Type Of Bird And Description - Document the species name and any special markings or features.

4. Bird's Action - Record sounds and activities while observing the bird.

5. Habitat - Document the bird's surroundings (forest, grasslands, wetland, etc.), nesting area, water source, and more.

6. Notes - Space to write additional information.

7. Bird Photo or Sketch - Space to place a photo or draw a picture of the bird.

DATE _____

LOCATION _____

TIME _____

WEATHER

TYPE OF BIRD & DESCRIPTION

BIRD'S ACTIONS

HABITAT

NOTES

BIRD PHOTO OR SKETCH

DATE _____

LOCATION _____

TIME _____

WEATHER

TYPE OF BIRD & DESCRIPTION

_____
_____
_____
_____
_____
_____

BIRD'S ACTIONS

_____
_____
_____
_____
_____
_____

HABITAT

_____
_____
_____
_____
_____
_____
_____

NOTES	BIRD PHOTO OR SKETCH

DATE_____
LOCATION_____
TIME_____

WEATHER

TYPE OF BIRD & DESCRIPTION

BIRD'S ACTIONS

HABITAT

NOTES

BIRD PHOTO OR SKETCH

DATE _____
LOCATION _____
TIME _____

WEATHER

TYPE OF BIRD & DESCRIPTION

BIRD'S ACTIONS

HABITAT

NOTES

BIRD PHOTO OR SKETCH

DATE _____

LOCATION _____

TIME _____

WEATHER

TYPE OF BIRD & DESCRIPTION

_____

BIRD'S ACTIONS

_____

HABITAT

_____

NOTES

_____

BIRD PHOTO OR SKETCH

DATE _____
LOCATION _____
TIME _____

WEATHER

TYPE OF BIRD & DESCRIPTION

BIRD'S ACTIONS

HABITAT

NOTES

BIRD PHOTO OR SKETCH

DATE_____
LOCATION_____
TIME_____

WEATHER

TYPE OF BIRD & DESCRIPTION

BIRD'S ACTIONS

HABITAT

NOTES

BIRD PHOTO OR SKETCH

DATE _____
LOCATION _____
TIME _____

WEATHER

TYPE OF BIRD & DESCRIPTION

BIRD'S ACTIONS

HABITAT

NOTES

BIRD PHOTO OR SKETCH

DATE _____
LOCATION _____
TIME _____

WEATHER

TYPE OF BIRD & DESCRIPTION

BIRD'S ACTIONS

HABITAT

NOTES

BIRD PHOTO OR SKETCH

DATE _____
LOCATION _____
TIME _____

WEATHER

TYPE OF BIRD & DESCRIPTION

BIRD'S ACTIONS

HABITAT

NOTES

BIRD PHOTO OR SKETCH

DATE _____

LOCATION _____

TIME _____

WEATHER

TYPE OF BIRD & DESCRIPTION

BIRD'S ACTIONS

HABITAT

NOTES

BIRD PHOTO OR SKETCH

DATE _____
LOCATION _____
TIME _____

WEATHER

TYPE OF BIRD & DESCRIPTION

BIRD'S ACTIONS

HABITAT

NOTES

BIRD PHOTO OR SKETCH

DATE _____
LOCATION _____
TIME _____

WEATHER

TYPE OF BIRD & DESCRIPTION

BIRD'S ACTIONS

HABITAT

NOTES

BIRD PHOTO OR SKETCH

DATE _____

LOCATION _____

TIME _____

WEATHER

TYPE OF BIRD & DESCRIPTION

BIRD'S ACTIONS

HABITAT

NOTES

BIRD PHOTO OR SKETCH

DATE _____
LOCATION _____
TIME _____

WEATHER

TYPE OF BIRD & DESCRIPTION

BIRD'S ACTIONS

HABITAT

NOTES

BIRD PHOTO OR SKETCH

DATE _____
LOCATION _____
TIME _____

WEATHER

TYPE OF BIRD & DESCRIPTION

BIRD'S ACTIONS

HABITAT

NOTES

BIRD PHOTO OR SKETCH

DATE _____
LOCATION _____
TIME _____

WEATHER

TYPE OF BIRD & DESCRIPTION

BIRD'S ACTIONS

HABITAT

NOTES

BIRD PHOTO OR SKETCH

DATE _____

LOCATION _____

TIME _____

WEATHER

TYPE OF BIRD & DESCRIPTION

BIRD'S ACTIONS

HABITAT

NOTES

BIRD PHOTO OR SKETCH

DATE _____
LOCATION _____
TIME _____

WEATHER

TYPE OF BIRD & DESCRIPTION

BIRD'S ACTIONS

HABITAT

NOTES

BIRD PHOTO OR SKETCH

DATE _____
LOCATION _____
TIME _____

WEATHER

TYPE OF BIRD & DESCRIPTION

BIRD'S ACTIONS

HABITAT

NOTES

BIRD PHOTO OR SKETCH

DATE_____
LOCATION_____
TIME_____

WEATHER

TYPE OF BIRD & DESCRIPTION

BIRD'S ACTIONS

HABITAT

NOTES

BIRD PHOTO OR SKETCH

DATE_____
LOCATION_____
TIME_____

WEATHER

TYPE OF BIRD & DESCRIPTION

BIRD'S ACTIONS

HABITAT

NOTES

BIRD PHOTO OR SKETCH

DATE _____
LOCATION _____
TIME _____

WEATHER

TYPE OF BIRD & DESCRIPTION

BIRD'S ACTIONS

HABITAT

NOTES

BIRD PHOTO OR SKETCH

DATE_____

LOCATION_____

TIME_____

WEATHER

TYPE OF BIRD & DESCRIPTION

BIRD'S ACTIONS

HABITAT

NOTES

BIRD PHOTO OR SKETCH

DATE _____
LOCATION _____
TIME _____

WEATHER

TYPE OF BIRD & DESCRIPTION

BIRD'S ACTIONS

HABITAT

NOTES

BIRD PHOTO OR SKETCH

DATE_____   WEATHER
LOCATION_____
TIME_____

TYPE OF BIRD & DESCRIPTION

_____
_____
_____
_____
_____
_____

BIRD'S ACTIONS

_____
_____
_____
_____
_____
_____

HABITAT

_____
_____
_____
_____
_____
_____

NOTES

_____
_____
_____
_____
_____
_____
_____
_____
_____
_____
_____
_____
_____
_____

BIRD PHOTO OR SKETCH

DATE_____
LOCATION_____
TIME_____

WEATHER

TYPE OF BIRD & DESCRIPTION

BIRD'S ACTIONS

HABITAT

NOTES

BIRD PHOTO OR SKETCH

DATE _____

LOCATION _____

TIME _____

WEATHER

TYPE OF BIRD & DESCRIPTION

BIRD'S ACTIONS

HABITAT

NOTES

BIRD PHOTO OR SKETCH

DATE _____

LOCATION _____

TIME _____

WEATHER

TYPE OF BIRD & DESCRIPTION

BIRD'S ACTIONS

HABITAT

NOTES

BIRD PHOTO OR SKETCH

DATE _____
LOCATION _____
TIME _____

WEATHER

TYPE OF BIRD & DESCRIPTION

BIRD'S ACTIONS

HABITAT

NOTES

BIRD PHOTO OR SKETCH

DATE _____
LOCATION _____
TIME _____

WEATHER

TYPE OF BIRD & DESCRIPTION

BIRD'S ACTIONS

HABITAT

NOTES

BIRD PHOTO OR SKETCH

DATE _____

LOCATION _____

TIME _____

WEATHER

TYPE OF BIRD & DESCRIPTION

BIRD'S ACTIONS

HABITAT

NOTES

BIRD PHOTO OR SKETCH

DATE _____
LOCATION _____
TIME _____

WEATHER

TYPE OF BIRD & DESCRIPTION

BIRD'S ACTIONS

HABITAT

NOTES

BIRD PHOTO OR SKETCH

DATE_____

LOCATION_____

TIME_____

WEATHER

TYPE OF BIRD & DESCRIPTION

BIRD'S ACTIONS

HABITAT

NOTES

BIRD PHOTO OR SKETCH

DATE _____
LOCATION _____
TIME _____

WEATHER

TYPE OF BIRD & DESCRIPTION

BIRD'S ACTIONS

HABITAT

NOTES

BIRD PHOTO OR SKETCH

DATE _____

LOCATION _____

TIME _____

WEATHER

TYPE OF BIRD & DESCRIPTION

BIRD'S ACTIONS

HABITAT

NOTES

BIRD PHOTO OR SKETCH

DATE _____
LOCATION _____
TIME _____

WEATHER

TYPE OF BIRD & DESCRIPTION

BIRD'S ACTIONS

HABITAT

NOTES

BIRD PHOTO OR SKETCH

DATE_____

LOCATION_____

TIME_____

WEATHER

TYPE OF BIRD & DESCRIPTION

BIRD'S ACTIONS

HABITAT

NOTES

BIRD PHOTO OR SKETCH

DATE_____
LOCATION_____
TIME_____

WEATHER

TYPE OF BIRD & DESCRIPTION

BIRD'S ACTIONS

HABITAT

NOTES

BIRD PHOTO OR SKETCH

DATE_____

LOCATION_____

TIME_____

WEATHER

TYPE OF BIRD & DESCRIPTION

_____
_____
_____
_____
_____
_____

BIRD'S ACTIONS

_____
_____
_____
_____
_____
_____

HABITAT

_____
_____
_____
_____
_____
_____

NOTES

_____
_____
_____
_____
_____
_____
_____
_____
_____
_____
_____
_____

BIRD PHOTO OR SKETCH

DATE_____
LOCATION_____
TIME_____

WEATHER

TYPE OF BIRD & DESCRIPTION

BIRD'S ACTIONS

HABITAT

NOTES

BIRD PHOTO OR SKETCH

DATE _____

LOCATION _____

TIME _____

WEATHER

TYPE OF BIRD & DESCRIPTION

BIRD'S ACTIONS

HABITAT

NOTES

BIRD PHOTO OR SKETCH

DATE _____
LOCATION _____
TIME _____

WEATHER

TYPE OF BIRD & DESCRIPTION

BIRD'S ACTIONS

HABITAT

NOTES

BIRD PHOTO OR SKETCH

DATE _____
LOCATION _____
TIME _____

WEATHER

TYPE OF BIRD & DESCRIPTION

BIRD'S ACTIONS

HABITAT

NOTES

BIRD PHOTO OR SKETCH

DATE_____
LOCATION_____
TIME_____

WEATHER

TYPE OF BIRD & DESCRIPTION

BIRD'S ACTIONS

HABITAT

NOTES

BIRD PHOTO OR SKETCH

DATE _____
LOCATION _____
TIME _____

WEATHER

TYPE OF BIRD & DESCRIPTION

BIRD'S ACTIONS

HABITAT

NOTES

BIRD PHOTO OR SKETCH

DATE_____
LOCATION_____
TIME_____

WEATHER

TYPE OF BIRD & DESCRIPTION

BIRD'S ACTIONS

HABITAT

NOTES

BIRD PHOTO OR SKETCH

DATE_____

LOCATION_____

TIME_____

WEATHER

TYPE OF BIRD & DESCRIPTION

BIRD'S ACTIONS

HABITAT

NOTES

BIRD PHOTO OR SKETCH

DATE _____

LOCATION _____

TIME _____

WEATHER

TYPE OF BIRD & DESCRIPTION

_____
_____
_____
_____
_____
_____

BIRD'S ACTIONS

_____
_____
_____
_____
_____
_____

HABITAT

_____
_____
_____
_____
_____
_____

NOTES

_____
_____
_____
_____
_____
_____
_____
_____
_____
_____
_____
_____
_____

BIRD PHOTO OR SKETCH

DATE_____
LOCATION_____
TIME_____

WEATHER

TYPE OF BIRD & DESCRIPTION

BIRD'S ACTIONS

HABITAT

NOTES

BIRD PHOTO OR SKETCH

DATE_____
LOCATION_____
TIME_____

WEATHER

TYPE OF BIRD & DESCRIPTION

BIRD'S ACTIONS

HABITAT

NOTES

BIRD PHOTO OR SKETCH

DATE_____   WEATHER
LOCATION_____
TIME_____

TYPE OF BIRD & DESCRIPTION
_____
_____
_____
_____
_____

BIRD'S ACTIONS
_____
_____
_____
_____
_____
_____

HABITAT
_____
_____
_____
_____
_____
_____

NOTES

BIRD PHOTO OR SKETCH

DATE _____
LOCATION _____
TIME _____

WEATHER

TYPE OF BIRD & DESCRIPTION

BIRD'S ACTIONS

HABITAT

NOTES

BIRD PHOTO OR SKETCH

DATE _____
LOCATION _____
TIME _____

WEATHER

TYPE OF BIRD & DESCRIPTION

BIRD'S ACTIONS

HABITAT

NOTES

BIRD PHOTO OR SKETCH

DATE _____
LOCATION _____
TIME _____

WEATHER

TYPE OF BIRD & DESCRIPTION

BIRD'S ACTIONS

HABITAT

NOTES

BIRD PHOTO OR SKETCH

DATE _____

LOCATION _____

TIME _____

WEATHER

TYPE OF BIRD & DESCRIPTION

_____
_____
_____
_____
_____
_____

BIRD'S ACTIONS

_____
_____
_____
_____
_____
_____

HABITAT

_____
_____
_____
_____
_____
_____

NOTES

BIRD PHOTO OR SKETCH

DATE_____

LOCATION_____

TIME_____

WEATHER

TYPE OF BIRD & DESCRIPTION

BIRD'S ACTIONS

HABITAT

NOTES

BIRD PHOTO OR SKETCH

DATE_____

LOCATION_____

TIME_____

WEATHER

TYPE OF BIRD & DESCRIPTION

_____
_____
_____
_____
_____
_____

BIRD'S ACTIONS

_____
_____
_____
_____
_____
_____

HABITAT

_____
_____
_____
_____
_____
_____

NOTES

BIRD PHOTO OR SKETCH

DATE _____
LOCATION _____
TIME _____

WEATHER

TYPE OF BIRD & DESCRIPTION

BIRD'S ACTIONS

HABITAT

NOTES

BIRD PHOTO OR SKETCH

DATE _____
LOCATION _____
TIME _____

WEATHER

TYPE OF BIRD & DESCRIPTION

BIRD'S ACTIONS

HABITAT

NOTES

BIRD PHOTO OR SKETCH

DATE_____
LOCATION_____
TIME_____

WEATHER

TYPE OF BIRD & DESCRIPTION

BIRD'S ACTIONS

HABITAT

NOTES

BIRD PHOTO OR SKETCH

DATE_____
LOCATION_____
TIME_____

WEATHER

TYPE OF BIRD & DESCRIPTION

BIRD'S ACTIONS

HABITAT

NOTES

BIRD PHOTO OR SKETCH

DATE _____
LOCATION _____
TIME _____

WEATHER

TYPE OF BIRD & DESCRIPTION

BIRD'S ACTIONS

HABITAT

NOTES

BIRD PHOTO OR SKETCH

DATE_____

LOCATION_____

TIME_____

WEATHER

TYPE OF BIRD & DESCRIPTION

_____
_____
_____
_____
_____
_____

BIRD'S ACTIONS

_____
_____
_____
_____
_____
_____

HABITAT

_____
_____
_____
_____
_____
_____

NOTES

BIRD PHOTO OR SKETCH

DATE _____
LOCATION _____
TIME _____

WEATHER

TYPE OF BIRD & DESCRIPTION

BIRD'S ACTIONS

HABITAT

NOTES

BIRD PHOTO OR SKETCH

DATE_____

LOCATION_____

TIME_____

WEATHER

TYPE OF BIRD & DESCRIPTION

BIRD'S ACTIONS

HABITAT

NOTES

BIRD PHOTO OR SKETCH

DATE _____

LOCATION _____

TIME _____

WEATHER

TYPE OF BIRD & DESCRIPTION

BIRD'S ACTIONS

HABITAT

NOTES

BIRD PHOTO OR SKETCH

DATE_____

LOCATION_____

TIME_____

WEATHER

TYPE OF BIRD & DESCRIPTION

BIRD'S ACTIONS

HABITAT

NOTES

BIRD PHOTO OR SKETCH

DATE _____
LOCATION _____
TIME _____

WEATHER

TYPE OF BIRD & DESCRIPTION

BIRD'S ACTIONS

HABITAT

NOTES

BIRD PHOTO OR SKETCH

DATE_____
LOCATION_____
TIME_____

WEATHER

TYPE OF BIRD & DESCRIPTION

_____
_____
_____
_____
_____
_____

BIRD'S ACTIONS

_____
_____
_____
_____
_____
_____
_____

HABITAT

_____
_____
_____
_____
_____
_____
_____

NOTES

_____

BIRD PHOTO OR SKETCH

DATE _____
LOCATION _____
TIME _____

WEATHER

TYPE OF BIRD & DESCRIPTION

BIRD'S ACTIONS

HABITAT

NOTES

BIRD PHOTO OR SKETCH

DATE _____
LOCATION _____
TIME _____

WEATHER

TYPE OF BIRD & DESCRIPTION

BIRD'S ACTIONS

HABITAT

NOTES

BIRD PHOTO OR SKETCH

DATE _____
LOCATION _____
TIME _____

WEATHER

TYPE OF BIRD & DESCRIPTION

BIRD'S ACTIONS

HABITAT

NOTES

BIRD PHOTO OR SKETCH

DATE_____

LOCATION_____

TIME_____

WEATHER

TYPE OF BIRD & DESCRIPTION

BIRD'S ACTIONS

HABITAT

NOTES

BIRD PHOTO OR SKETCH

DATE _____
LOCATION _____
TIME _____

WEATHER

TYPE OF BIRD & DESCRIPTION

BIRD'S ACTIONS

HABITAT

NOTES

BIRD PHOTO OR SKETCH

DATE _____

LOCATION _____

TIME _____

WEATHER

TYPE OF BIRD & DESCRIPTION
_____
_____
_____
_____
_____
_____

BIRD'S ACTIONS
_____
_____
_____
_____
_____
_____

HABITAT
_____
_____
_____
_____
_____
_____
_____

NOTES

BIRD PHOTO OR SKETCH

DATE _____
LOCATION _____
TIME _____

WEATHER

TYPE OF BIRD & DESCRIPTION

BIRD'S ACTIONS

HABITAT

NOTES

BIRD PHOTO OR SKETCH

DATE _____

LOCATION _____

TIME _____

WEATHER

TYPE OF BIRD & DESCRIPTION

_____
_____
_____
_____
_____
_____

BIRD'S ACTIONS

_____
_____
_____
_____
_____
_____

HABITAT

_____
_____
_____
_____
_____
_____

NOTES

_____
_____
_____
_____
_____
_____
_____
_____
_____
_____
_____
_____
_____
_____
_____
_____
_____

BIRD PHOTO OR SKETCH

DATE_____

LOCATION_____

TIME_____

WEATHER

TYPE OF BIRD & DESCRIPTION

BIRD'S ACTIONS

HABITAT

NOTES

BIRD PHOTO OR SKETCH

DATE _____

LOCATION _____

TIME _____

WEATHER

TYPE OF BIRD & DESCRIPTION

BIRD'S ACTIONS

HABITAT

NOTES

BIRD PHOTO OR SKETCH

DATE_____
LOCATION_____
TIME_____

WEATHER

TYPE OF BIRD & DESCRIPTION

BIRD'S ACTIONS

HABITAT

NOTES

BIRD PHOTO OR SKETCH

DATE _____
LOCATION _____
TIME _____

WEATHER

TYPE OF BIRD & DESCRIPTION

BIRD'S ACTIONS

HABITAT

NOTES

BIRD PHOTO OR SKETCH

DATE_____
LOCATION_____
TIME_____

WEATHER

TYPE OF BIRD & DESCRIPTION

BIRD'S ACTIONS

HABITAT

NOTES

BIRD PHOTO OR SKETCH

DATE_____

LOCATION_____

TIME_____

WEATHER

TYPE OF BIRD & DESCRIPTION

BIRD'S ACTIONS

HABITAT

NOTES

BIRD PHOTO OR SKETCH

DATE _____
LOCATION _____
TIME _____

WEATHER

TYPE OF BIRD & DESCRIPTION

BIRD'S ACTIONS

HABITAT

NOTES

BIRD PHOTO OR SKETCH

DATE _____

LOCATION _____

TIME _____

WEATHER

TYPE OF BIRD & DESCRIPTION

BIRD'S ACTIONS

HABITAT

NOTES	BIRD PHOTO OR SKETCH

DATE _____
LOCATION _____
TIME _____

WEATHER

TYPE OF BIRD & DESCRIPTION

BIRD'S ACTIONS

HABITAT

NOTES

BIRD PHOTO OR SKETCH

DATE_____
LOCATION_____
TIME_____

WEATHER

TYPE OF BIRD & DESCRIPTION

BIRD'S ACTIONS

HABITAT

NOTES

BIRD PHOTO OR SKETCH

DATE _____

LOCATION _____

TIME _____

WEATHER

TYPE OF BIRD & DESCRIPTION

BIRD'S ACTIONS

HABITAT

NOTES

BIRD PHOTO OR SKETCH

DATE _____
LOCATION _____
TIME _____

WEATHER

TYPE OF BIRD & DESCRIPTION

BIRD'S ACTIONS

HABITAT

NOTES

BIRD PHOTO OR SKETCH

DATE _____

LOCATION _____

TIME _____

WEATHER

TYPE OF BIRD & DESCRIPTION

BIRD'S ACTIONS

HABITAT

NOTES

BIRD PHOTO OR SKETCH

DATE_____
LOCATION_____
TIME_____

WEATHER

TYPE OF BIRD & DESCRIPTION

BIRD'S ACTIONS

HABITAT

NOTES

BIRD PHOTO OR SKETCH

DATE _____
LOCATION _____
TIME _____

WEATHER

TYPE OF BIRD & DESCRIPTION

BIRD'S ACTIONS

HABITAT

NOTES

BIRD PHOTO OR SKETCH

DATE_____
LOCATION_____
TIME_____

WEATHER

TYPE OF BIRD & DESCRIPTION

BIRD'S ACTIONS

HABITAT

NOTES

BIRD PHOTO OR SKETCH

DATE _____
LOCATION _____
TIME _____

WEATHER

TYPE OF BIRD & DESCRIPTION

BIRD'S ACTIONS

HABITAT

NOTES

BIRD PHOTO OR SKETCH

DATE_____
LOCATION_____
TIME_____

WEATHER

TYPE OF BIRD & DESCRIPTION

BIRD'S ACTIONS

HABITAT

NOTES

BIRD PHOTO OR SKETCH

DATE _____
LOCATION _____
TIME _____

WEATHER

TYPE OF BIRD & DESCRIPTION

BIRD'S ACTIONS

HABITAT

NOTES

BIRD PHOTO OR SKETCH

DATE _____
LOCATION _____
TIME _____

WEATHER

TYPE OF BIRD & DESCRIPTION

BIRD'S ACTIONS

HABITAT

NOTES

BIRD PHOTO OR SKETCH

DATE_____
LOCATION_____
TIME_____

WEATHER

TYPE OF BIRD & DESCRIPTION

_____
_____
_____
_____
_____
_____

BIRD'S ACTIONS

_____
_____
_____
_____
_____
_____

HABITAT

_____
_____
_____
_____
_____
_____

NOTES

_____
_____
_____
_____
_____
_____
_____
_____
_____
_____
_____
_____
_____
_____
_____

BIRD PHOTO OR SKETCH

DATE_____
LOCATION_____
TIME_____

WEATHER

TYPE OF BIRD & DESCRIPTION

BIRD'S ACTIONS

HABITAT

NOTES

BIRD PHOTO OR SKETCH

DATE _____
LOCATION _____
TIME _____

WEATHER

TYPE OF BIRD & DESCRIPTION

BIRD'S ACTIONS

HABITAT

NOTES

BIRD PHOTO OR SKETCH